The Countries

Iran

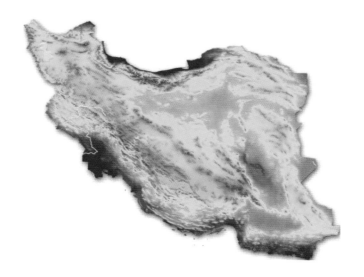

Bob Italia
ABDO Publishing Company

visit us at
www.abdopub.com

Published by ABDO Publishing Company, 4940 Viking Drive, Edina, Minnesota 55435.
Copyright © 2001 by Abdo Consulting Group, Inc. International copyrights reserved in all countries. No part of this book may be reproduced in any form without written permission from the publisher.

Printed in the United States.

Photo Credits: Corbis

Contributing Editors: Tamara L. Britton and Kate A. Furlong
Art Direction & Maps: Neil Klinepier

Special thanks to Oaktai Goglani for his invaluable help with the Persian language.

Library of Congress Cataloging-in-Publication Data

Italia, Bob, 1955-
　　Iran / Bob Italia.
　　　　p. cm. -- (The countries)
　　Includes index.
　　ISBN 1-57765-495-1
　　　　1. Iran--Juvenile literature. [1. Iran.] I. Title. II. Series.

DS254.75 .I83 2001
955--dc21

00-050430

Contents

Salam!.. 4

Fast Facts 6

Timeline 7

History 8

The Land 12

Plants & Animals 18

The People 20

Earning a Living 26

Where They Live 28

From Here to There 30

The Government 32

Holidays & Festivals 34

Fun in Iran 36

Glossary 38

Web Sites 39

Index 40

Salam!

Hello from Iran! Iran is one of the world's oldest countries. Most of Iran's land is mountain and desert. Its climate varies from region to region.

Persians make up more than half of Iran's population. Iran's official language is also Persian. Almost all Iranians are Muslims.

Iran is one of the world's leading oil producers. Many Iranians work in service industries. Iran also has farming, manufacturing, and construction businesses.

Teheran (tay-RAHN) is the capital of Iran. It is Iran's largest city and its commercial center. Most of Iran's rural villages are farming communities.

Iran's government is based on **Islamic** law. So Iranians celebrate religious as well as national holidays. They spend much of their leisure time visiting friends and relatives. They also enjoy a variety of sports.

Salam *from Iran!*

Fast Facts

OFFICIAL NAME: Jomhuri-ye Eslami-ye Iran
  (Islamic Republic of Iran)
CAPITAL: Teheran

LAND
- Mountain Ranges: Elburz and Zagros Mountains
- Highest Peak: Mount Damavand 18,386 feet (5,604 m)
- Major Deserts: Dasht-e Kavir and Dasht-e Lut
- Major River: Karun
- Largest Lake: Urmia

PEOPLE
- Population: 74,644,000 (2000 est.)
- Major Cities: Teheran, Meshed, Esfahan, Tabriz
- Language: Persian
- Religion: Islam

GOVERNMENT
- Form: Islamic Republic
- Head of State: President
- Legislature: Majles
- National Anthem: "Soroude Jomhuri-ye Eslami-ye Iran"
  ("Anthem of the Islamic Republic of Iran")
- Nationhood: About 700 B.C.

ECONOMY
- Agriculture: Wheat, sugar beets, rice, barley, nuts
- Fishing: Caviar
- Manufacturing: Petroleum products, textiles, cement,
  brick, food products
- Mining Products: Petroleum
- Money: Rial (ten dinars equal one rial)

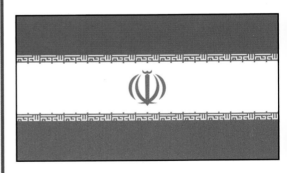

Iran's Flag

Timeline

3000s B.C.	Elamites arrive in Iran
1500s B.C.	Aryans arrive in Iran
728-550 B.C.	Medes rule Iran
550 B.C.	Cyrus the Great conquers Iran
300s B.C.	Alexander the Great conquers Iran
A.D. 637	Muslim Arabs conquer Iran
1055	Turks take control of Iran
1925	Reza Khan becomes shah
1941	Mohammed Reza Pahlavi becomes shah
1979	Revolutionaries take control of Iran's government; Ayatollah Khomeini becomes Iran's new leader
1980-1990	Iran-Iraq War

Iranian women spending rials in the marketplace

History

Iran's recorded history begins with the Elamites. They were a group of settlers who arrived in Iran in about 3000 B.C. About a thousand years later, another group of settlers arrived in Iran. They were called the Aryans.

The mixing of the Elamites and the Aryans created three main tribes. These tribes were the Medes, the Parthians, and the Persians.

The Medes ruled the land from 728 to 550 B.C. Then a Persian named Cyrus the Great overthrew the Medes. The Persians established a mighty empire.

The Greek ruler Alexander the Great conquered Iran in the 300s B.C. Then several other groups seized control of the land. In A.D. 637, Iran was conquered by the Arabs. They introduced **Islam** to Iran.

The Turks overthrew the Arabs in 1055. For the next seven hundred years, many different groups controlled the country. Then in 1925, a man named Reza Khan declared himself **shah**. Reza Shah reorganized the government, formed a strong military, and created more schools.

Reza Shah

Reza Shah's son, Mohammed Reza Shah Pahlavi, took control of the country in 1941. He continued his father's programs to make Iran more modern. Some of his programs upset Iran's **Islamic** population.

Islamic rebels overthrew the shah in 1979. A few weeks later, Ayatollah Ruhollah Khomeini became Iran's new leader. He formed a new **republic** based on the Islamic religion.

In 1980, Iran was attacked by its neighbor Iraq. Iraq wanted to seize Iranian land that was rich in oil. Iraq's attack led to the Iran-Iraq War. Iran remained in control of its land. But thousands of people died before the war ended in 1990.

Today, **reform** groups have gained power in Iran's government. They are fighting for more personal freedoms and less government control in the daily lives of Iranian citizens.

Opposite page: Ayatollah Ruhollah Khomeini

The Land

Iran lies in southwestern Asia, northeast of the Arabian **Peninsula**. The country faces Armenia, Azerbaijan, the Caspian Sea, and Turkmenistan on the north. It faces Afghanistan and Pakistan on the east. The Persian Gulf and the Gulf of Oman lie to the south. Iraq and Turkey border Iran on the west.

Iran is divided into four major land regions. They are the interior **plateau**, the mountains, the Caspian Sea coast, and the Khuzistan Plain.

The interior plateau lies in central and eastern Iran. It covers half the country's total area. The plateau stands about 3,000 feet (900 m) above sea level. Much of the plateau is two large, **uninhabited** deserts, the Dasht-e Kavir and the Dasht-e Lut. These deserts cover more than 38,000 square miles (98,000 sq km).

The Elburz and the Zagros Mountains surround most of the interior **plateau**. Iran's highest peak is Mount Damavand. It rises 18,386 feet (5,604 m) in the Elburz range.

The Zagros Mountains run from the borders of Turkey and Azerbaijan to the Persian Gulf. Wide, fertile valleys are in the northern and central parts of the range.

Mount Damavand

Rainfall

★TEHERAN

AVERAGE YEARLY RAINFALL

Inches		_Centimeters_
Under 10		Under 25
10 - 20		25 - 50
20 - 40		50 - 100

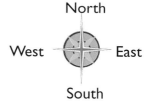

North

West — East

South

Temperature

Winter

★TEHERAN

AVERAGE TEMPERATURE

Fahrenheit		_Celsius_
Over 86°		Over 30°
68° - 86°		20° - 30°
50° - 68°		10° - 20°
32° - 50°		0° - 10°
14° - 32°		-10° - 0°

Summer

TEHERAN

The Caspian Sea coast is a narrow strip of low-lying land. It is between the Caspian Sea and the slopes of the Elburz Mountains.

The Khuzistan Plain lies between the border of Iraq and the Zagros Mountains. The region has Iran's richest **petroleum** deposits. The Khuzistan Plain is also an important agricultural area. Iran's largest river, the Karun, runs through it.

Iran's climate varies from region to region. In the mountainous areas, severe winters are followed by mild summers. The plains have extremely hot and humid summers. Winters on the plains are mild and pleasant.

Opposite page: An Iranian woman wearing a chador and a roupush swims in the Caspian Sea.

Plants & Animals

Iran has few forests. Most are found in the Caspian Region. Evergreens and **deciduous** trees grow well there. These forests are home to cheetahs and tigers. Birds such as pheasants, seagulls, ducks, and geese also live in the Caspian Region.

The Zagros Mountains are covered by trees such as oak, elm, and maple. Leopards, bears, hyenas, wild boars, goats, gazelles, and wild sheep live in the wooded mountains.

Sand dunes in Iran's deserts have thick patches of shrubs. Tamarisk, date palms, fig trees, and myrtle grow in desert **oases**. Animals of the desert include buzzards, lizards, and snakes.

Two Iranian women walk near fig trees in a desert.

The People

Most of Iran's land is mountain and desert. Most Iranians live along the Caspian Sea coast and in the capital city, Teheran.

More than half of the Iranian people are **descendants** of an Asian people called the Aryans. Persians are the largest Aryan **ethnic** group. They make up more than half of Iran's population. Most Persians live in central Iran or on the slopes of the surrounding mountains.

The official language of Iran is Persian. It is also called Farsi (FAHR-see). Most of the people speak Persian. It is used in the schools and in all official government communications.

Iranian law requires all children ages 7 to 13 to attend school. But some children still do not go. Most of these children are girls who live in Iran's rural villages. Higher education in Iran includes colleges and universities. It also has technical, **vocational**, and teacher-training schools.

Iranian children in school

Almost all Iranians are Muslims. Most belong to the Shiite branch of **Islam**. It is Iran's state religion.

About 250,000 Baha'is make up Iran's largest religious minority. Iran also has Christians, Jews, and followers of an ancient Persian religion called Zoroastrianism (ZOHR-uh-WAHS-tree-uh-NEH-zehm).

City housing includes modern apartment buildings and traditional houses. Most rural families live in traditional houses. The houses are made of mud or unbaked brick and have thatched or flat mud roofs.

Some of Iran's rural people are nomads. They travel across the countryside with their sheep, goats, and other livestock to seasonal grazing areas. The nomads live in round, black felt tents.

Traditional houses are small mud or brick buildings surrounded by high walls. Each house opens onto a central courtyard.

An Iranian waiter serves trays of food.

Most of the men in Iran's cities wear Western-style clothing. Women wear long veils called *chadors* (CHAW-dorz) over their heads. They wear a coat-like garment called a *roupush* (roo-POOSH) over their clothing.

The main foods of the Iranian people are rice and bread. A traditional Iranian dish is *abgusht* (ab-GUSHT). It is a thick soup made with meat and beans. *Dolmeh* (DOHL-meh) is another popular dish. It is vegetables stuffed with meat and rice. Iran is famous for its kebabs. Kebabs are roasted meat served on a skewer. Popular beverages include tea and a yogurt drink called *dough* (DOH).

Beef Kebab

2 pounds rib-eye steak
1 large onion

1/2 cup olive oil
salt and pepper

Cut the steak into one-inch cubes. Peel the onion and slice it thin. Layer the onion and the beef cubes in a bowl. Cover and refrigerate for 6 to 24 hours.

Remove the beef cubes from the bowl. Put them on skewers. Hit the kebabs with a meat tenderizer to flatten the beef cubes. Pour the olive oil over the kebabs. Salt and pepper both sides, and barbecue to taste.

AN IMPORTANT NOTE TO THE CHEF: Always have an adult help with the preparation and cooking of food. Never use kitchen utensils or appliances without adult permission and supervision.

English	Persian
Yes	Baleh (BAH-lay)
No	Nah (NAH)
Thank You	Mamnoon am (mam-NOON am)
Please	Lotfan (LOHT-fan)
Hello	Salam (sah-LAHM)
Goodbye	Khoda hafez (koh-DAH hah-fehz)
Mother	Madar (mah-DAR)
Father	Pehdar (pay-DAR)

LANGUAGE

Earning a Living

The Iran-Iraq War of the 1980s greatly hurt Iran's **economy**. But slowly the economy has improved. Today, Iranians work in many different fields.

The oil industry is important to Iran's economy. Iran is the world's third-largest oil exporter. The National Iranian Oil Company is owned by the government. It operates Iran's oil industry.

Farming is difficult in Iran. Poor soil and lack of water make growing crops difficult. Land that is fit for farming is planted with wheat, barley, rice, fruit trees, vegetables, and nuts.

Almost half of all Iranians work in service industries. They work in places such as government agencies, hospitals, and schools. Other Iranians manufacture goods. They produce bricks, cement, food products, and **petroleum** products.

An oil refinery in Iran

Where They Live

Teheran is Iran's capital and largest city. It is located in north-central Iran. Teheran is home to more than nine million people.

Teheran is divided into an old section and a new section. The old section is home to many **mosques** (mahsks) and a traditional bazaar. At the bazaar, visitors can buy food, spices, carpets, and gold jewelry. Teheran's new section has businesses and modern homes.

Meshed is Iran's second-largest city. It is located in eastern Iran. Meshed is home to the Holy Shrine. It is Iran's most holy **Islamic** site. Many people make **pilgrimages** to Meshed to visit the Holy Shrine.

Rural Iran has many farming villages. These villages often have a small, central square and wide streets. A mosque and a public bath are often near the square.

A rural village in Iran

From Here to There

Iran's rugged land has made it difficult and expensive to develop a modern system of transportation. Only about a third of the country's roads are paved.

Most Iranians in the cities travel by bus. In rural areas, bicycles, donkeys, horses, and mules are important means of transportation.

The government owns the country's rail system and airline. Iran Air's planes fly within Iran and to some foreign countries. The country's main airport is in Teheran.

Most of Iran's trade travels in and out of Persian Gulf ports. Kharg Island in the Persian Gulf is the country's chief oil-exporting port.

Two women travel by donkey in rural Iran.

The Government

Iran is an Islamic **republic**. Its laws are based on the religion of **Islam**. The Supreme Leader makes sure that Iran's government follows Islamic principles. He has the final say in all areas of Iran's government.

Iranians elect a president who may serve two four-year terms. The president oversees the day-to-day operations of the government.

The Majles (MAHJ-less) is Iran's lawmaking body. It is made up of 270 members. They are elected to the Majles for four-year terms. Members of the Majles pass Iran's laws.

The Council of Guardians reviews the laws passed by the Majles. Twelve people serve on this council. They make sure the laws do not violate Islamic principles or Iran's **constitution**.

The opening ceremony of the new Majles building in March 2001

Holidays & Festivals

Iranians celebrate many religious and national holidays. Iran's major holiday is Nowruz (no-ROOZ), the Iranian New Year. Nowruz begins on the first day of spring. It lasts 13 days.

During Nowruz, people make an arrangement on their tables. The arrangement has seven small dishes of fruits, wheat sprouts, and a bowl of water in which a goldfish swims. Together with a mirror and several painted eggs, the arrangement is called Haft-Sin (HAFT-seen).

People spend the first few days of Nowruz visiting nearby friends and relatives. On the last day of the Nowruz celebration, many Iranians go on picnics.

Major religious events include Ramadan, a month of fasting from dawn to dusk. There is also Eid-é Fetr (ay-dee FEH-ter), the festival that marks the end of Ramadan.

Ghadir-é Khom (GHAH-dray khom) honors both the birthday of the **prophet** Mohammed and the day that Mohammed appointed Emam Ali his successor.

The Magnificent Victory of the **Islamic** Revolution of Iran honors the anniversary of Ayatollah Khomeini's coming to power in 1979. The Heart-Rending Departure of the Great Leader of the Islamic Republic of Iran honors Khomeini's death.

A Haft-Sin

Fun in Iran

Iranians spend much of their leisure time visiting one another and entertaining friends and relatives in their homes. They also enjoy a variety of sports, including basketball, soccer, volleyball, and weight lifting.

Many men practice a traditional form of weight lifting exercises and gymnastics at athletic clubs called *zurkhanehs*. The word *zurkhaneh* means house of strength.

The National Museum of Iran houses a collection of ceramics, stone figures, and carvings dating from around 4000 B.C. The Reza Abbasis Museum contains examples of **Islamic** painting, pottery, and jewelry. The National Palace Museum was once the **shah's** palace. It is now a complex of museums.

Opposite page: The Iranian soccer team celebrates winning the Hussein Cup.

In Teheran people may also visit the busy Emam Khomeini **Mosque**, the Armenian Sarkis Cathedral, and its parks and gardens.

Glossary

constitution - the laws that govern a state or nation.

deciduous - trees that lose their leaves in the fall.

descendant - a person who is related to a certain group of ancestors.

economy - the way a nation uses its money, goods, and natural resources.

ethnic - a way to describe a group of people who have certain things in common, such as language, culture, history, race, or national origin.

Islam - a religion based on the teachings of Mohammed as they are written in the Koran. People who follow Islam are called Muslims.

mosque - a Muslim place of worship.

oasis - a place in the desert that is fertile because it has a source of water.

peninsula - land that sticks out into water and is connected to a larger land mass.

petroleum - a thick, yellowish-black oil. It is used to make gasoline.

pilgrimage - a journey to a holy place.

plateau - a raised area of flat land.

prophet - a religious leader who speaks as the voice of God.

reform - to change something, usually making it better.

republic - a form of government in which power lies with the people and elected officials and not a king or queen.

shah - the title of a ruler in Iran.

uninhabited - a place where nothing lives.

vocational - a school that provides training in a skill, trade, or occupation.

Web Sites

Salam Iran
http://www.salamiran.org/
This Web site is sponsored by the Iranian embassy in Ottawa, Canada. It has great information on Iran's economy, culture, and religion. A special section on women includes features on traditional women's clothing, art, and much more!

Presidency of the Islamic Republic of Iran
http://www.president.ir/
This is the official site for the president of Iran. Visitors to this site can read a biography of Iran's president and read the latest presidential news.

Iranian Cultural & Information Center
http://persia.org/
This site offers a wealth of information on Iran. Visitors can find Iranian recipes, listen to Iranian music, and view images from Iran.

These sites are subject to change. Go to your favorite search engine and type in "Iran" for more sites.

Index

A
Alexander the Great
      8
animals 18, 22, 30

C
children 20, 21
climate 4, 16
clothing 24
culture 34, 36
Cyrus the Great 8

D
deserts 4, 12, 18, 20

E
economy 4, 26
education 20, 21

F
farming 4, 16, 26
food 24, 26, 28, 34

G
geography 4, 12, 14,
      16, 18, 20, 30
government 4, 10, 20,
      26, 30, 32

H
holidays 4, 34, 35
housing 22, 28

I
Iran-Iraq War 10, 26

K
Khomeini, Ruhollah
      10, 35

L
language 4, 20
leisure 4, 36

M
Meshed 28
Mohammed 35
mountains 4, 14, 16,
      18, 20
museums 36

O
oil 4, 10, 26, 30

P
plants 18

R
religion 4, 8, 10, 22, 28,
      32, 34
Reza Kahn 9, 10
Reza Shah Pahlavi 10

S
sports 4, 36

T
Teheran 4, 20, 28, 30,
      37
transportation 30